RISK
FORWARD

RISK
FORWARD

EMBRACE THE UNKNOWN
AND UNLOCK YOUR HIDDEN GENIUS

VICTORIA LABALME

HAY HOUSE, INC.

Carlsbad, California • New York City
London • Sydney • New Delhi

Published in the United States by: Hay House, Inc.: www.hayhouse.com®
Published in Australia by: Hay House Australia Pty. Ltd.: www.hayhouse.com.au
Published in the United Kingdom by: Hay House UK, Ltd.: www.hayhouse.co.uk
Published in India by: Hay House Publishers India: www.hayhouse.co.in

Cover Design: Ashley Zink and Victoria Labalme
Interior Design: Victoria Labalme
Interior Illustrations: Copyright © 2021 by Victoria Labalme
Cover and Interior Layout: Bryn Starr Best

Cataloging-in-Publication Data is on file at the Library of Congress

Hardcover ISBN: 978-1-4019-6180-0

E-book ISBN: 978-1-4019-6181-7

Audiobook ISBN: 978-1-4019-6269-2

10 9 8 7 6 5 4 3 2 1

1st edition, March 2021

Printed in the United States of America

SUSTAINABLE FORESTRY INITIATIVE
Certified Chain of Custody
Promoting Sustainable Forestry
www.sfiprogram.org
SFI-01268

SFI label applies to the text stock

for my godmother, Elizabeth,

for my family, friends, and clients . . .

and
most of all
for
YOU

Some people in life know exactly what they want to achieve.

This is a book for the rest of us.

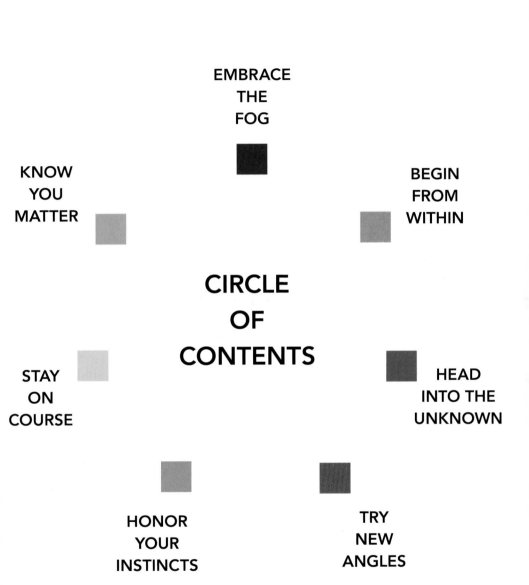

EMBRACE
THE
FOG

KNOW
YOU
MATTER

BEGIN
FROM
WITHIN

CIRCLE
OF
CONTENTS

STAY
ON
COURSE

HEAD
INTO THE
UNKNOWN

HONOR
YOUR
INSTINCTS

TRY
NEW
ANGLES

CONTENTS

■ EMBRACE THE FOG

■ BEGIN FROM WITHIN

■ HEAD INTO THE UNKNOWN

■ TRY NEW ANGLES

HONOR YOUR INSTINCTS

STAY ON COURSE

KNOW YOU MATTER

Many of the insights here are collected from my years in the performing arts.

These ideas have helped me in my work and in my life and have also helped thousands of entrepreneurs, executives, and individuals.

I hope you will find value in them too.

HOW TO READ THIS BOOK

You can read the sections of this book in any order and at any pace, and if one part doesn't speak to you, choose another. Focus on those that resonate.

These are doorways in . . . and doorways out . . . and will have a different effect on you from year to year. Each time you return, you will discover something new.

Consider this book a touchstone for your soul—and a playbook in the improvisation of your work and life.

HOW TO USE THIS BOOK

Wherever you see this image,

it means there are extra resources available.

These can be accessed at:

www.RiskForward.com/Resources

They offer stories, videos, journal pages, and "how to" steps to help you Risk Forward and put these ideas into practice—either on your own or with others.

However, if you're looking for a "step-by-step formula"

you won't find it there . . . or here

because there is no formula outside of you.

<u>You</u> are the formula.

NOT
KNOWING

For many years, I suffered under a myth that unless I was clear and had a plan, I could not succeed.

I often made choices that others thought were odd; I seemed to veer off from the path people expected, and I couldn't always explain why except that it seemed right . . . for me.

When I chose to go out West for college vs. stay back East near home, my mother thought I might be defecting from the family.

When I chose to study theater vs. law, my mother thought I might be defecting from life.

When my classmates signed up for graduate school, I signed up for a 75-day expedition into the Alaskan wilderness.

When all my friends started getting married and having babies, I stayed single. If anyone questioned me, I would simply respond, "I skipped my first divorce."

And when everyone seemed to have one clear career path—in medicine, law, or business—I explored a variety of interests in the performing arts—writing, acting, comedy, dancing, directing, filmmaking, and mime.

Mime? YES. Mime.

People began to ask, "What exactly are you doing? Where is all this going?"

The truth was, I didn't know, and because I had no clear answer, I started to feel "less than"—like I was falling behind and falling short. I started to wonder, *Does everyone else have a map to life? Where was I the day they gave out the maps?*

Nonetheless, I kept following what interested me and lit me up even though I wasn't sure where it would lead.

I supported myself by production managing theater events and producing corporate training videos.

Little by little, my performing arts career began to grow. I started acting in commercials; I landed small parts on television; the venues for my one-woman shows got bigger; and the invitations more prestigious.

I was on my way.

Then, early one morning in September 2001, I looked out my kitchen window in lower Manhattan to see a black gash in one of the World Trade Center towers. A trail of smoke drifted horizontally into the blue sky. Moments later, a fireball exploded from the second tower . . . followed by the slow mushroom cloud implosion of both buildings and the disintegration of life as we knew it.

Two days later, my mother was diagnosed with pancreatic cancer.

With Ground Zero still smoldering outside my window, I tried to process the news that in a few months my mother would be gone.

I found myself in a profound phase of uncertainty, a cloud of not knowing. And I started asking myself the questions so many of us do when our world spirals into crisis:

I took care of my mom. I volunteered at Ground Zero. And I searched for ways to use my arts background to help others.

And then, like a glimmer of light, seemingly out of nowhere, I got a call from an event coordinator who had seen me perform in a comedy club years before.

He explained that he was in charge of the upcoming convention for the National Speakers Association, and he invited me to open the event.

Excited by the possibility that I could contribute, I said, "Yes." And so I took a section of my one-woman show and customized it for that specific audience.

Surrendering to this opportunity and heading into the unknown changed the course of my life and career.

That appearance led me to help speakers with their messaging and storytelling skills;

and *that* in turn inspired me to create communication workshops for different organizations.

That ultimately led me to design and deliver keynotes for larger audiences.

Who would have thought

. . . that I would be sharing principles from the performing arts to help people improve their work and their lives

. . . that I would be coaching thousands of people to express their ideas in their own unique way

. . . that I would be consulting CEOs on their communication strategy

. . . all while running my own company?

. . . and who would have thought that I would fall in love with a man 20 years older and get married late in life?

It certainly surprised me.

All along, I had simply taken the next step, not knowing where it would lead. I had followed what lit me up. And it lit other people up.

As I continued giving keynotes and workshops in different countries, I became acutely aware of something: people so often spoke about the importance of clarity, goals, and decisiveness, but in hallways or over lunch, many would lean in and whisper to me that they were unsure of their decisions, direction, or next steps. They felt wrong for not knowing, as if it was something to hide.

And yet I had discovered through my years in the arts that it is in this very gap between what is and what could be that we find our way; it is here that some of our best ideas are born. As I began to address this topic, more people started asking for guidance.

And so in private one-on-one sessions, then in larger events, I began to help people navigate through the Fog of Not Knowing to discover their own original path forward.

THE FOG

In each of our lives at various points along the way, we find ourselves in the Fog of Not Knowing—a period of transition, when the path, the plan, or the project is not yet clear.

It could be that you're in the midst of a business or creative endeavor, evaluating options and figuring out next steps.

It could be that you're leading a team into new territory or you're keen to try something new but don't yet have the courage.

It could be that you've been shaken unexpectedly from your past due to changes in the world, in your relationships, or with your health and you now find yourself in an unfamiliar realm.

It's possible, too, that nothing externally has changed, but internally there's been a shift. Your perspective is now different. The tectonic plates of your inner landscape have adjusted, and old ways of thinking will no longer do.

Regardless of how you arrive in this place, you now find yourself in the Fog of Not Knowing where you can't quite see what's next.

This period "in between"—whether for minutes or for months—is to be respected and honored; it is fertile and full of promise.

If you can meet this void without grasping for the most convenient way out, what you discover will be beyond your expectations and imagination.

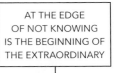

AT THE EDGE
OF NOT KNOWING
IS THE BEGINNING OF
THE EXTRAORDINARY

THE TRUTH

THE TRUTH THAT NO ONE TELLS YOU

There's a secret that successful individuals rarely share. And it is this . . .

Some of the most celebrated companies and creative endeavors didn't start with complete clarity, a detailed plan, or a five-year goal. They started with an idea, a wisp, a glimmer of a thought, which the person then followed and explored, often through significant periods of self-doubt.

Clarity is not the place from which we begin but rather the place at which we ultimately arrive. And it is a cycle we go through again and again—sometimes in the span of minutes, sometimes in the span of months, sometimes in the span of years.

The more original our path forward, the stronger the forces will be that rise up against it.

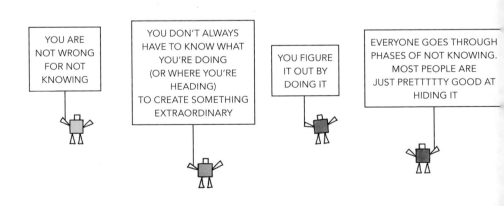

YOU ARE NOT WRONG FOR NOT KNOWING

YOU DON'T ALWAYS HAVE TO KNOW WHAT YOU'RE DOING (OR WHERE YOU'RE HEADING) TO CREATE SOMETHING EXTRAORDINARY

YOU FIGURE IT OUT BY DOING IT

EVERYONE GOES THROUGH PHASES OF NOT KNOWING. MOST PEOPLE ARE JUST PRETTTTTY GOOD AT HIDING IT

FORCES

There are many forces that can hold you back.

VOICES

We live in a world that prizes decisiveness, planning, goal setting, and clarity.

People often ask . . .

"What's the plan?"
"What's your goal?"
"Where do you want to be in one year, three years, or five?"

They like to say . . .

"Just make a decision."
"You need to be clear."
"If you don't know where you're going, you'll never get there."

Though intended to be helpful, when you're in the delicate phase of discovery, comments of this nature actually make things worse.

COMPARISONS

It may appear that others around us are accomplishing more, doing "it" better, or moving faster.

The lurking fear is that if we don't keep up, we're going to lose out.

We can fall into the trap of "Compare and Despair," powering down, becoming deflated, depressed, convinced that we don't know enough or have enough . . .

Alternatively, we can shift into a phase of hyperactivity, making fast decisions, generating a spree of busyness just to be doing something.

The pressure to do more, be more, and grow more continues, all based on the assumption that more is better . . .

It can start to feel like quicksand.

The more we scramble, the more we sink.

PRESSURES

The pressures come from every corner . . .

THE PRESSURE	THE EFFECT
THE PRESSURE OF TIME	RUSHING AND WORRYING, THINKING WE DON'T HAVE ENOUGH
THE PRESSURE TO CONFORM	SHAVING OFF PARTS OF WHO WE TRULY ARE TO FIT INTO A MOLD
THE PRESSURE TO KEEP UP	RUNNING AND "DOING" BECAUSE EVERYONE ELSE IS
THE PRESSURE TO BE GREAT	HYPER-EXTENDING OURSELVES FOR RECOGNITION OR TO PROVE SOMETHING
THE PRESSURE NOT TO BE GREAT	DOWNPLAYING OUR SUCCESSES SO AS NOT TO MAKE OTHERS JEALOUS
THE PRESSURE TO BE HAPPY	FEIGNING HAPPINESS, WHICH ULTIMATELY MAKES US FEEL MORE HOLLOW
THE PRESSURE TO FULFILL ONE'S POTENTIAL	FEELING LIKE NO MATTER WHAT WE DO, IT'S NEVER ENOUGH

KEEPING UP

Our days can start to feel like a conveyor belt of never-ending activities.

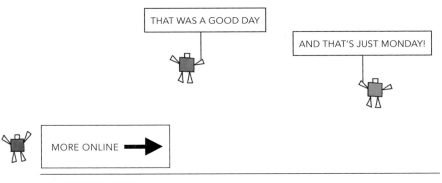

SLEEP – WAKE UP – MEDITATE – CHECK MESSAGES – WAKE UP KIDS – CHECK POSTS, TEXTS, SOCIAL CHANNELS – GET UNDRESSED – GET IN THE SHOWER – GET DRESSED – GET COFFEE – GET KIDS READY FOR SCHOOL – CHECK MESSAGES AGAIN – GET TO WORK – DOWNLOAD FILES – UPLOAD FILES – CHECK SPREADSHEETS AND REPORTS – DEAL WITH DEADLINES – PRINT, SIGN, SCAN, SEND – EAT LUNCH IN FRONT OF COMPUTER – CHEW WHILE CHECKING E-MAIL – CHECK MESSAGES – ATTEND MEETINGS, MORE MEETINGS, MEETINGS ABOUT MEETINGS – HANDLE E-MAILS AND CONFERENCE CALLS – REVIEW REPORT – CONNECT WITH COLLEAGUE – CHECK E-MAIL – FINISH DOCUMENT – ATTEND ANOTHER MEETING – GET SOME EXERCISE – BICYCLE, TREADMILL, PILATES, PILATES – BICEPS, BICEPS, TRICEPS, ABS – CHECK BODY IN MIRROR – DO SOME YOGA TO CALM DOWN – BREATHE – HEAD HOME – PICK UP GROCERIES – UNPACK GROCERIES – HAVE DINNER WITH FAMILY – CHECK MESSAGES AND POSTS AGAIN – GET IN BED – WATCH A SHOW – CALL FRIEND – READ BOOK ON SPIRITUALITY – CHECK MESSAGES ONE MORE TIME – AND GO TO SLEEP

THAT WAS A GOOD DAY

AND THAT'S JUST MONDAY!

MORE ONLINE ➡

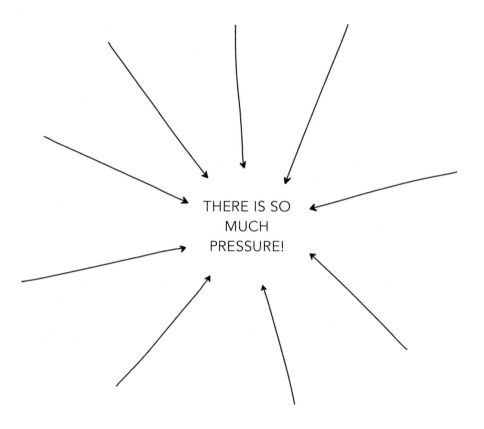

THERE IS SO
MUCH
PRESSURE!

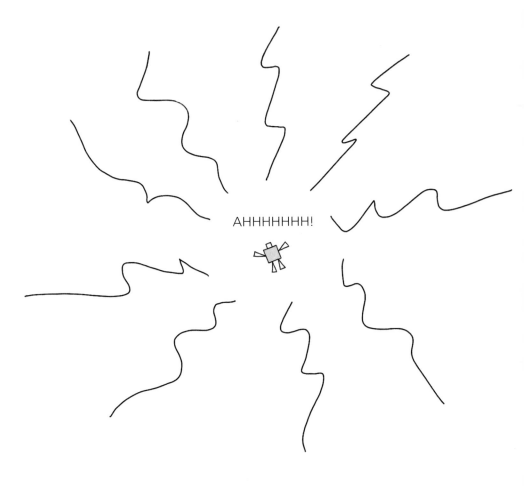

There is a way out.

RISKING
FORWARD

Years ago I studied movement with the legendary mime art-ist Marcel Marceau. There was a technique he used when he walked forward, an approach he called "Risque Avant":

. . . to be present, balance forward, heart open.

The position of "Risque Avant" resembled the sail of a boat, arched open with the wind.

It was a way of moving that made you feel almost like you were being pulled forward, and over time, I've come to think of this very much as a philosophy for life and work:

how we can move forward,

    a little off balance,

        heart open,

            heading into the unknown.

YOUR
INNER
CURRENT

BEGIN FROM WITHIN

Within each of us is an inner line of wisdom, an Inner Current that runs through everything we do.

It is in your cells and in your soul . . .

It is what motivates you from the inside out.

And whether you're aware of it or not, this inner line, this invisible silent force, shows up in every area of your life.

For many people, it's unconscious, yet you are expressing it every day.

And when you're at your best, you're most closely aligned with it.

Like

. . . the current in a river

. . . the energy in an electrical wire

. . . the life force rising through a tree

it is as much a part of you as all things nature . . .

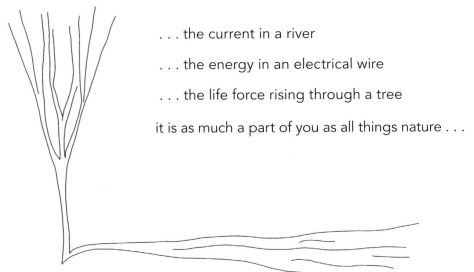

HOW YOU KNOW YOU'RE ON IT

Even if you can't identify or articulate your Inner Current, you know you're connected to it when you're feeling . . .

Intrigued

Engaged

Curious

Propelled

Pulled forward

Energized

Electrified

Calm

Grounded

Centered

Expansive

Inspired

Whole

Razzed

Fired up

Emboldened

Activated

Alive

. . . and even a little "Excitedly scared"

HOW YOU KNOW YOU'RE OFF IT

You know you're disconnected from
your Inner Current when you're feeling . . .

Lifeless

Static

Bored

Drained

Disjointed

Uninterested

Disconnected

Constricted

Frazzled

Dull

Overwhelmed

Fractured

Scattered

Depressed

Despairing

Dejected

Flattened

Empty

Hopeless

No doubt, even if you're on course, there are times in your life

when you will face unexpectedly tough periods.

You will have obligations to fulfill that can

be daunting and can drain you.

Even projects you had been excited about

can lead you at times to feel low.

But if day after day

you're not feeling motivated

maybe it's *not* because there's

something wrong with you;

maybe it's because

the path you're on

isn't

your

path.

SO HOW DO I FIND THAT PATH?
AND WHAT REALLY MATTERS ANYWAY?

THE
DESERTED
ISLAND

WHAT REALLY MATTERS

One way to connect with your Inner Current is to remember what really matters . . . for you.

When I first made the transition from performing arts to public speaking and was looking for how best to express what I wanted to say, a booking agent asked me a question that helped distill my message into its most essential form.

It also helped me understand for myself the unseen driving force that ran through everything I did—my Throughline.

Over the years I've adapted and refined this experience into what I call the Deserted Island Question.

I have since shared it with hundreds of thousands of people around the globe to help them start to identify their own Inner Current and recognize the times in their lives when their actions and beliefs felt most aligned.

THE DESERTED ISLAND QUESTION

If you were on a deserted island dying
and you knew you weren't going to make it . . .
that this was the end . . .

but there was a young person there with you—
someone you cared about deeply . . .

and if—before you died—
you could give that young person
only one piece of advice about life
and how they might best live theirs . . .

what would that one piece of advice be?

YOUR DESERTED ISLAND ANSWER

Whatever just came into your heart/mind/soul
is exactly right for you
and is the beginning of the essence of your
Inner Current.

It's the driving force behind your vision,
your voice, and your values.
It is what you believe really matters . . .
and what calls you to Risk Forward.

OTHER PEOPLE'S ANSWERS

These are just a few of the many responses I've received from people around the world:

- "Be kind"
- "Don't hold back"
- "Serve other people"
- "Give without expectation"
- "Live for something bigger than yourself"
- "Learn from everything and share with others"
- "Love what you do and do what you love"
- "Surround yourself with people who raise your game"
- "Always keep your enthusiasm and ambition"
- "Use your strengths to help others"
- "Remember that kindness and respect will open many doors"
- "Be true to yourself"
- "Work hard; play harder"
- "Give your best"
- "Learn to let go"
- "Make the world a better place"
- "Enjoy every day"

WHAT WAS YOURS?

YOUR EVERYDAY INTERACTIONS

Your Deserted Island Answer has a profound influence on your day-to-day actions, even in the smallest of ways.

Think, for a moment, of your life like a movie. Within it there are different scenes.

A scene might be

- A call
- A conversation
- An event
- A meeting
- A meal with others

In any given scene, you have an opportunity to express your Deserted Island Answer.

If your answer is "Be kind," how can you be kind on the call?

If your answer is "Don't hold back," how can you share your ideas at the meeting?

If your answer is "Use your strengths to help others," how can you engage your gifts for the larger good?

When you look back and reflect on the moments when you felt most "on course," you will notice that your actions were in some way an expression of your Deserted Island Answer.

Staying closely aligned with this will help you Risk Forward; it will keep you connected to what matters most to you.

MORE ONLINE ➡️

4
QUESTIONS

Your responses to these four questions

will help you clarify your next move

and keep you risking forward in the right direction.

1. WHAT INTERESTS YOU NOW?

At one point in my career, I took a workshop with Remy Charlip, a well-known performer, director, dancer, and the author of various children's books my sister and I had grown up reading and loving.

On the opening day, 15 of us arrived—a bit excited and a bit nervous.

Remy explained that we'd start by each introducing ourselves, but he added this guideline. "Don't tell us what you've done. Tell us what interests you **now**."

One by one, we went around the room, saying, "I'm interested in . . ." For the next few weeks, that was all we knew of one another. Not each other's credentials, not who someone had been before, but what interested them now, in this moment.

It was phenomenally freeing.

Remy didn't want us relying on our ego or judging other people for their past. He gave us the opportunity to arrive in the class as newborns.

The fact is, our pasts can hold us back—not just our failures but our successes too.

WHAT INTERESTS YOU NOW?

MORE ONLINE ➡️

2. WHAT LIGHTS YOU UP?

What do you love doing? What brings you joy?

- Helping people succeed?
- Standing up for a cause?
- Building a top-notch team?
- Being onstage . . . or on camera?
- Hosting events?
- Making complex concepts simple?
- Bringing a plan to life?
- Raising a family?
- Taking care of those in need?
- Writing music?
- Creating art?

WHAT BRINGS YOU JUICE?

How can you do this even in small ways . . . or large?

WHAT FIRES YOU UP?

MORE ONLINE ➡

3. WHAT STOPS TIME FOR YOU?

Bob Dylan said that the purpose of art is to stop time.

Art can indeed "stop time." When you're watching your favorite show, captivated by a photograph, reading an extraordinary book, engrossed in a film, or being transported by a piece of music, time passes without your awareness. You're off the crazy busy conveyor belt of a day.

Our work has similar potential.

Certain activities can place us in a different temporal realm—editing a piece of text, hosting an event, writing code, coaching clients, analyzing data, seeing patients, developing a flow chart, leading a team, teaching a course, playing an instrument, cooking for friends, reading a book . . .

What activities cause hours to pass without your noticing?

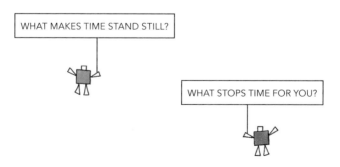

4. WHAT DON'T YOU WANT?

When a clear picture of where we're heading has not yet come into view, we're usually able to articulate a few elements regarding what we DON'T want.

My grandfather used to say, "Good judgment comes from experience and experience comes from bad judgment."

The clarity that ensues from prior unpleasant experiences can propel us forward.

So . . .

- What don't you want?

- What won't you put up with?

- What situations are no longer acceptable to you?

Sometimes risking forward requires you to say "No"—no to what you've done before; no to what is presented or offered; no to what others think you should do; no to something you had thought you wanted for so long but now is no longer right.

This takes courage—and often more than simply saying, "Yes."

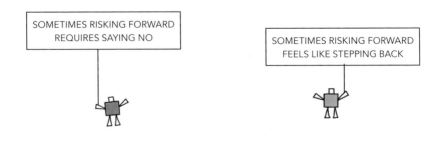

SOMETIMES RISKING FORWARD
REQUIRES SAYING NO

SOMETIMES RISKING FORWARD
FEELS LIKE STEPPING BACK

THE CRIMSON STAR

FOLLOW
INTEREST, CURIOSITY, EXCITEMENT

Trust that light that flickers across your soul

. . . even if it makes no sense to others

. . . even if people question or discourage you.

Your interest, curiosity, and excitement

are not only "good enough" reasons

to explore an idea.

They are THE reasons.

They are your Hidden Genius at work,

and they carry more wisdom than you know.

It is not until we've had the courage to step into the unknown

and head toward what I call the Crimson Star

that we discover where we are next meant to go.

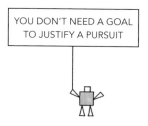

YOU DON'T NEED A GOAL
TO JUSTIFY A PURSUIT

THE CRIMSON STAR

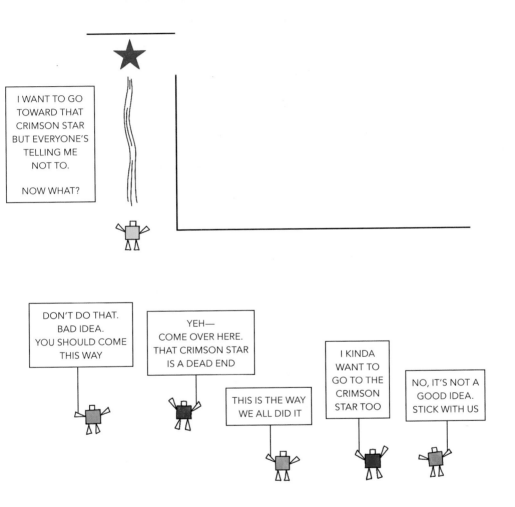

I'M GOING ANYWAY

BAAAAD IDEA

BIG MISTAKE

WISH I HAD THE COURAGE TO DO THAT TOO

I WANT TO GO

NAHHH. STICK WITH US

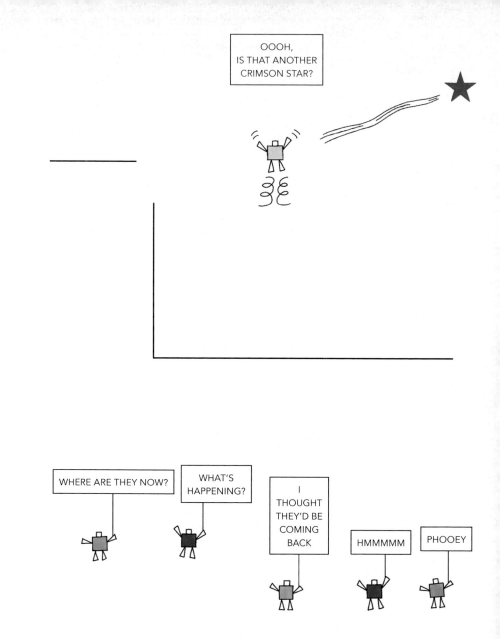

THE
NEXT STEP

JUST TAKE THE NEXT STEP

YOU DON'T ALWAYS HAVE TO KNOW

WHERE IT'S GOING

  OR

    HOW IT WILL TURN OUT

      OR

        WHAT YOU'LL USE IT FOR

          OR

            WHY YOU'RE EVEN DOING IT

              . . . EXCEPT THAT IT SEEMS INTERESTING OR FUN.

YOU NEVER KNOW WHERE
SOMETHING COULD LEAD

SOMETIMES ONLY THE
NEXT STEP IS REVEALED

START SMALL

My sister, Lisa Osterland, started her artistic path by following a barely perceptible impulse.

For years, she had been an elementary school teacher in the Boston area, and when she and her husband and young kids moved to Montreal, she put a pause on her teaching career to focus on her family. She didn't know what was next.

Then, one evening, as her two sons were quietly doing their homework at the kitchen table, Lisa went to the cabinet that housed the pencils, rulers, and other homework supplies. There she saw a tiny three-inch-by-two-inch mounted canvas—a leftover prize from a birthday party.

The urge to paint on the canvas took over. Lying nearby happened to be a photo of their townhouse, so Lisa decided to use that as her subject. By dinnertime, the house was sketched and the first touches of paint were applied. The final result was not a masterpiece, but it was certainly something unusual.

It became the very first "pocket painting," and it inspired Lisa to make many more. She eventually developed a thriving business called Pocket Paintings—paintings that literally fit in your pocket.

*

For years my friend Stu McLaren had been consulting entre-preneurs in marketing and business development.

Growing his business, however, felt slow and heavy. It was challenging to stand out from other experts in his field.

A mentor, Reid Tracy, suggested Stu concentrate on one specific aspect of his expertise—helping people launch, grow, and scale membership sites, something Stu knew a great deal about from his years running a software company supporting this niche.

At first, Stu was hesitant. Reducing his consulting practice to one area felt risky. It seemed like the pool of potential clients would be much smaller, and he'd be eliminating a big portion of his market. And, as the primary provider for a family with two children at home, he knew that if this venture didn't work out, he'd face a lot of financial pressure.

But for a long time, Stu had been sensing something inside that he couldn't deny. So he risked forward. He started small, hosting a workshop for just 15 people. That led to requests for additional workshops; then an online course; then a live conference. And in less than five years, Stu's company, TRIBE, bloomed into a multimillion-dollar enterprise attracting more clients than he had ever envisioned.

*

Years ago, Mellody Hobson shared a wonderful quote she had heard from Arianna Huffington, and I have never forgotten it. "Don't limit yourself to your imagination, because the world will bring you more than you can possibly imagine."

*

Odette D'Aniello grew up in Guam, where she had been a child laborer in a bakery. Although her life was difficult, one of the jobs she loved most was decorating cakes. Years later, when she moved to the States, she evaluated her options for a career. She considered academia and law, but neither seemed like the right fit; and then she remembered that decorating cakes had always been something she enjoyed. Although it was risky, she decided to open a tiny bakery with her family.

"I didn't know how to open a business; I didn't have a degree in business; and I didn't have a business plan. We didn't even know what a business plan was."

They started with a tiny cafe and painted the place themselves. "We literally held parts together with duct tape."

One cake led to the next and though there were difficult moments along the way, including a near bankruptcy, Odette kept going. Twenty-one years later, her company, Celebrity Gourmet Ventures, is still flourishing, distributing cakes in over 800 stores.

All along, Odette had followed her Inner Current and what lit her up. At an event I hosted, Odette shared her story, choking up: "We make judgments about people, and what motivates them. And we make judgments about ourselves. I've always had a kind of negative association with the bakery business, an emotional back and forth. I've wondered, 'Should I have been here? Was this the purpose of my life?' And I realize now that my business is not about cakes; it's about celebrating life's sweet moments."

The small steps we take are often in service of something far greater than we may recognize at the time.

INTUITION

Your choice may make no sense to others and even at times to yourself.

But there's a greater wisdom at work that has its own internal logic.

You may not understand why you're compelled to make a certain decision—and you can't always explain it—but when your Inner Current is buried, it shows up as intuition.

WORTH REPEATING:
WHEN YOUR INNER CURRENT
IS BURIED, IT SHOWS UP AS INTUITION

I WISH WE HAD A
SONOGRAM FOR OUR SOULS

SEEDS

EARLY IDEAS OFTEN LOOK ODD

As you start to explore your nascent ideas, they're often a little peculiar looking, a bit like a seed just starting to germinate.

In the early days above ground, sprouts are at their most vulnerable, and it's in this tender phase that outsiders most often start to ask questions.

- Why are you doing this?

- Who are you to do this?

- Is that the best use of your time?

- Are you sure it's going to work?

- How exactly will that make money?

- I don't get it. Why would someone be interested?

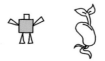

An early idea can so easily get dented, damaged, or destroyed.

A few years ago, I started an informal creative lab called the PAC—the Performing Arts Collective—so writers, performers, and comedians could try out new work in a safe environment.

Chris Wink, one the founders of Blue Man Group—the internationally acclaimed performance company—became an early PAC member. He'd been looking for a community in which to test new material without it getting crushed.

As Chris explained, Blue Man Group itself had started with a simple idea Chris had to make himself bald and blue and walk around New York City to see how people reacted.

One of the first people he dared tell this crazy notion to was his close friend Matt Goldman, who was working at a software company at the time. Chris wasn't expecting much more than a confused expression or a laugh, but what he got instead was "That sounds cool. Let's do it!"

And thus it began. Not long after, Phil Stanton joined as the third Blue Man.

They had no concept what this would turn out to become: a multimillion-dollar global enterprise.

So imagine if instead of saying, "That sounds cool," Matt had responded with, "That sounds weird. Why would you do that?"

Perhaps Blue Man Group might never have gone beyond that inkling Chris first had.

When you're in a delicate phase of discovery and finding the courage to Risk Forward, be careful with whom you share your early ideas. It's essential that they land in fertile soil, and you must protect the perimeter.

KEEP CLOSE THE PEOPLE WHO ENCOURAGE YOU TO EXPLORE YOUR IDEAS

WHAT IS IN YOU IS SOMETHING WE HAVE NEVER SEEN BEFORE

WHO ARE OTHERS TO SAY WHAT WE MIGHT OR MIGHT NOT BECOME?

IDEAS

TRUST THE IDEA THAT CAN LEAD TO THE IDEA

When we are developing a path, plan, or project—on our own or with others—it's easy to keep our ideas hidden if they're not fully formed, seemingly impractical, or in the minority. We don't speak up for fear of being judged; we opt instead to remain silent.

This is a loss for our communities, organizations, and those we serve and represent. It's also a loss for ourselves. Our voices and our visions matter.

Ideas arrive in your mind for a reason. They are gifts. You have the right—and in some cases even the responsibility—to speak up. One way to Risk Forward is to "Trust the idea that can lead to the idea."

If you're with others, you can simply say, "Okay, this may not be right, but it could be the idea that leads to the idea."

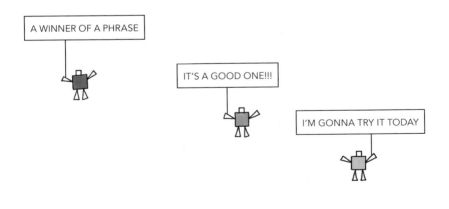

This statement immediately deflects potential judgment. It helps people who are listening to start looking for how your idea might inspire one of their own . . . what might be ignited within them by you.

Your ideas and insights matter. Trust them.

IDEA

THE

TO

LEAD

CAN

THAT

IDEA

THE

TRUST

IDEA

THE

TO

LEAD

CAN

THAT

IDEA

THE

TRUST

STUMBLING

STUMBLE FORWARD

In my first year at Stanford University, I signed up for a seminar called *Introduction to Reading and Writing Poetry*. On Day 1, our professor had us practice our critiquing skills.

For this he passed out a collection of poems, explaining that these were samples from last semester's students. Names had been removed to protect privacy.

He gave us a few moments to read. Heads bent, we sat in silence.

The poems were not good: confusing, derivative, and filled with what in the writing world is called "purple prose" —language that is cloying and overly ornate.

We practiced different ways to offer feedback, and about 20 minutes in, our professor paused the discussion.

"Great. So, do you know who wrote these poems?"

"Last year's students," we responded.

"Actually, these are the early poems of Robert Frost, Langston Hughes, Emily Dickinson . . ."

We were dumbfounded.

In an instant we were filled with optimism for our own potential.

Greatness rarely begins great.

CREATING

START WITHOUT A SCRIPT

Years ago, when I was just starting to put together a new one-woman show, I had a lot of ideas, but as yet no clarity on the direction the show might take. I was overwhelmed by all the options for how the material could be shaped and what the story line could be, and I felt undue pressure as people kept asking me what the show was going to be "about." I didn't know.

A theater friend offered to help. On three-by-five colored index cards, he had me write down each bit, story, or idea that was floating around in my mind—one idea per card. I did this over the course of a few days. Then we met. He took the collection of cards and hid them behind his back, shuffling the deck. One by one he flashed each card at me and studied my response.

"This one?" he asked.
I squished up my face.
He set it to the side.

"This one?"
I beamed.
He put it in a different area.

"This one?"
My chest sunk.
He put that card with the first.

"This one?"

I tilted my head sideways, shrugging my shoulders.

He put that card in a third zone.

About 10 minutes later, we had three piles:

DEFINITEs, MAYBEs, and **NOs**.

In a short amount of time, we had winnowed my ideas from 50 down to approximately 30.

We repeated this process, further reducing the deck, and then set the NOs aside.

Spreading the remaining cards out across the floor, we began to see patterns. Some ideas naturally grouped. Others were interesting but clearly belonged in another show. An internal logic started to make itself known.

After grouping and regrouping, arranging and rearranging, experimenting and testing out ideas, a show began to emerge.

Because I risked forward from a place of not knowing, without a script or a map, what arrived was far beyond anything I could have imagined or planned from the start.

Creativity doesn't happen in a line. The creative process is— by its very nature—one that happens *out of order.*

Over the years, I have developed this index card technique into a comprehensive "V-Card System" to help businesses and individuals discover patterns in their own work and find their way forward—executives planning projects, authors brainstorming books, experts prepping interviews, marketers planning launches, agencies developing pitches, entrepreneurs designing retreats, and speakers crafting presentations.

My clients find that it crystallizes their thinking, cuts their prep time in half, and is a lot of fun.

Clarity comes when we Risk Forward and remain open to surprising combinations and new ways of seeing.

MORE ONLINE ➡️

FEATURING

IF YOU CAN'T FIX IT, FEATURE IT

When I first started working in the corporate arena, I thought I needed to hide my background in the arts. I did whatever I could to cover it up: I wore suits; I adopted the business jargon; I presented my past experiences in a way that made them sound corporate.

But one of my early clients saw through it and exclaimed, "Victoria—it's because you're an artist that we hired you. You bring a perspective we don't get anywhere else."

And so I risked forward.

I stopped trying to "fix" my differences and instead began to "feature" them. I started using theater principles to teach sales strategies; I started sharing on-camera techniques to help executives deliver their messages more authentically; and I started illustrating my written materials with my little characters.

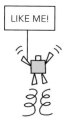

In an attempt to succeed and move ahead, we sometimes try to hide parts of who we really are.

In many cases, it's to our benefit to do the exact opposite.

IF YOU CAN'T FIX IT, FEATURE IT

- If you're new to a field, make that your advantage. "I bring a fresh perspective."

- If you've been around for a while, highlight that. "I offer a depth of experience that is rare."

- If you run your own operation, tell those you serve, "You won't be working with people I've trained. You'll be working directly with me."

Akira Armstrong, an extremely talented dancer and choreographer, had appeared as a background performer in high-profile videos and television shows. But when she went to audition for the lead in any project, she was told, "You're a great dancer, but we just don't know what to do with you." She didn't have the typical body type for the industry. Time after time she was turned away.

And so rather than try to "fix" herself to fit into a mold, she featured who she was and is. Out of rejection, she rose to new heights and created "Pretty BIG Movement"—a professional international dance company that features full-figured women.

Akira risked forward to break the norm of what had been done before, and in so doing, created a whole new lifestyle movement.

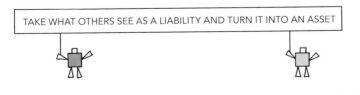

TAKE WHAT OTHERS SEE AS A LIABILITY AND TURN IT INTO AN ASSET

Kate Hutchison was chief marketing officer of a software company. At the request of the CEO, she rebranded a suite of products, but the changes she made upset the vast majority of the engineers and sales team members.

When we met to plan out her keynote for the company conference, we brainstormed a variety of options for how to acknowledge the issue. Kate settled on a bold approach.

As her opening, she stepped onstage, looked out at the audience of thousands, and said, "I know what you're thinking." She clicked to her first slide. There, in huge letters, was the acronym "WTF?"

The audience burst out laughing. They knew that she knew they were upset. In acknowledging what they were feeling, she began to rebuild trust and rapport.

INSTEAD OF HIDING AN ISSUE, RISK FORWARD AND FEATURE IT

FULL
SPECTRUM

THE PRISM EFFECT

When we don't see a reflection in the outside world of what we find within ourselves, the temptation is to hide parts of who we really are in order to fit into a mold.

But if you think of the metaphor of light shining through a prism, the prism reveals that white light is actually comprised of a full range of colors fused together.

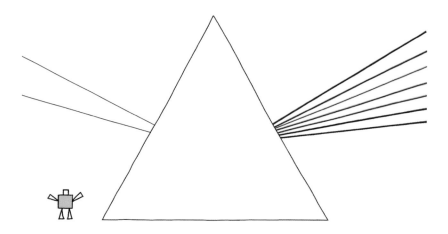

If you remove one of the colors, the light dims.

The same is true for you.

When you hide parts of who you are, you diminish your power. Conversely, when you embrace your "full spectrum"—your personality, your past, your passions, and your perspective— your strength increases.

And when you Risk Forward to fuse disparate elements together in unusual ways, even if you don't see an example represented in the world around you, you lead the way for others—in your industry, community, or culture.

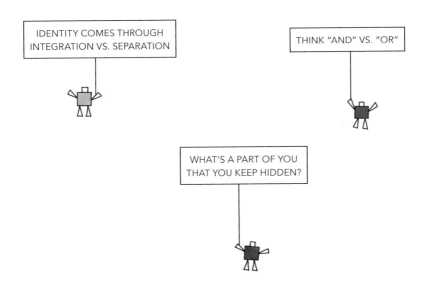

The Prism Effect can be applied to how we show up in the world as people and also to how we express our ideas.

Dr. Kathleen Pike, professor of psychology at Columbia University, opened an international mental health conference in London as the keynote speaker. In an effort to capture the audience's attention and tap into her unique perspective, she and I worked together to come up with an unexpected metaphor.

Years before, Kathleen had studied ikebana, the art of Japanese flower arranging. And so onstage, she demonstrated the art, creating a flower arrangement in front of the live audience and describing the essential contribution of each branch and the symbolic meaning of the flowers. When the arrangement was finished, she shared the most central precept in ikebana, but the part of ikebana that most people fail to see—the negative space. Kathleen spoke about how, when it comes to global health issues, mental health is like that negative space in the arrangement—invisible and overlooked.

Many attendees commented on this striking metaphor and said it was one of the most memorable keynotes they'd ever experienced. Kathleen got written up in journals and invited to other conferences to speak. She did what had not been done before.

Her Risk Forward paid off, and years later, her message lives on.

*

Ryan Levesque, CEO of The ASK Method Company, is an expert in helping business owners grow their companies. He also happens to love LEGO. It totally lights him up, and it's a big part of his life with his two sons.

Given that his work is highly analytical and data based, I encouraged Ryan to incorporate LEGO into his messaging as a way to better communicate his strategies, distinguish his brand, and have more fun.

Ryan was skeptical at first, concerned he might not be taken seriously. Ultimately, though, he took the risk and ran with the idea. He came up with a range of applications, one of which was this analogy:

As with LEGO, where you sometimes have to take apart what you've made to make something better, the same is true in business: sometimes you have to deconstruct what you've built to build something better.

Ryan's references to LEGO now show up in his stories, metaphors, and even conference stage sets. By fusing together two seemingly disparate elements—LEGO and marketing analytics—Ryan has increased the power of his messaging and differentiated his brand.

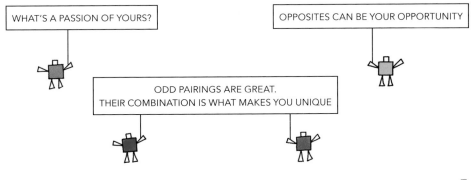

WHAT'S A PASSION OF YOURS?

OPPOSITES CAN BE YOUR OPPORTUNITY

ODD PAIRINGS ARE GREAT.
THEIR COMBINATION IS WHAT MAKES YOU UNIQUE

Move beyond the limits of what's been done before. Risk Forward to express yourself **the way only YOU can**. Here are some examples.

- The manager who loves poetry and starts her team meetings each Monday with a line from one of her favorite poets. People say it inspires them each week.

- The financial advisor who loves his Ducati motorcycle and parks it inside his office. When prospects arrive, they immediately get a glimpse into his style and personality. He sets himself apart from the stereotypical advisor before the meeting even begins.

- The strategic planning professor who loves comedy and starts each seminar with a comedic Top 10 list. Students rush to arrive on time so as not to miss the opening of his class.

- The health-care executive who loves art and uses examples from modern art as a metaphor to explain the way human cells interact.

- The administrative assistant who loves the Oscars and each year during Academy Awards week rolls out a red carpet beside her desk.

What's an outside passion, talent, or hobby of yours and how can you Risk Forward to bring it into your work—as an analogy, metaphor, story, demonstration, experience, prop, or point of distinction?

As the psychologist Rollo May said, the opposite of courage is not cowardice; it's conformity.

EMBRACE THE FULL SPECTRUM OF WHO YOU ARE

MORE ONLINE ➡

VULNERABILITY

THE UNTOLD STORY

Bill Watkins stepped onstage and took a big risk.

It was his turn at an event I hosted to help entrepreneurs and executives with their storytelling.

Looking out to the audience, Bill slowly reenacted a scene from 28 years before: he was sitting in a recliner in his living room in front of the fireplace . . . on the table next to him, a faded leather journal . . . and next to it, a bottle of Percocet.

He was starting to write a suicide note to his wife when his golden retriever came in and stared up at him. The two looked at each other for a very long time, and then Bill closed his journal, stood up, and put the Percocet back in the medicine cabinet. He couldn't commit suicide in front of his dog.

Bill was shaking as he recounted each moment. The other workshop participants sat motionless, transfixed. When he finished, Bill revealed that he'd never told that story to anyone, not even his wife.

He had stepped into the unknown, heart open.

Years later, Bill wrote me to say that sharing this story in front of a live audience cracked him open. It allowed him to drop the veneer he'd been keeping up as a business consultant. He started to be more himself—a bit more renegade, a bit more raw, a bit more vulnerable.

He now regularly shares this story with his clients—CEOs and small business owners, many of whom are vets and military academy alumni.

Bill's willingness to be more open allows them to connect on a whole new level. It also gives his clients the courage to tell their own stories and express more of who they really are in their business communications and branding.

Bill credits that moment onstage as the breakthrough that led to his company's rapid growth.

We never know where our Risk Forward will carry us . . . and others.

DISCOVERY

CREATING "INSIDE OUT" ... INSIDE OUT

When we're watching a movie, many of us might think that what we see onscreen is what the filmmakers intended to create from the start.

But at the wrap party for Pixar's film *Inside Out*—a screening for the cast and crew—the writer and director, Pete Docter, gave a brief speech, acknowledging people for all they had put into the project.

I was lucky enough to be a guest standing in the back of the room.

Toward the end of his remarks, Pete added, "I want to thank you for staying with us as we found the film."

The key phrase: " . . . *as we found the film.*"

Creative acts are not acts of knowing. They are acts of discovery.

Whether it's a new company or a new product, a new piece of software or a new work of art, a new venture in science, or a new path through life, when you are breaking new ground, there is no map even on a project as big as a multimillion-dollar feature film.

In Pete's words, "Any creative endeavor is a discovery. You start out with a gut sense that something feels worthwhile only to realize it's shallow and stale. Then you're lost for a while, not sure where to turn. Only by wrestling through countless rewrites and late nights of self-doubt do you find something new. You can't make a new discovery by following a preprinted map."

ORIGINAL WORK DOESN'T HAVE A MAP

ORIGINAL LIVES DON'T EITHER

VISION

CIRCLE OF CONFUSION

When I first studied filmmaking, I learned about a term for the visual effect when a lens has not yet fully found its focus.

It's called a "Circle of Confusion."

Our lives and projects are similar.

A NECESSARY PHASE. ON THE WAY TO CLARITY, WE OFTEN PASS THROUGH A PERIOD OF CONFUSION. IT'S NOT INHERENTLY BAD. IT'S

MORE ONLINE ➡️

DON'T OUTSOURCE YOUR VISION

When a vision is not yet clear, and when we're hesitant to Risk Forward, it's tempting to hand over the reins.

We want someone else to make the decisions. We want them to tell us what to do.

We assume that because we're not yet clear, we never will be.

Clarity is a process.

And sometimes the project, plan, or path tells *you* what *it* wants to be and at that point, it takes on a life of its own, and *it guides you.*

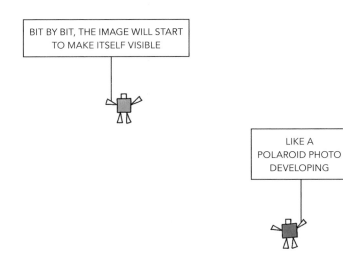

BIT BY BIT, THE IMAGE WILL START TO MAKE ITSELF VISIBLE

LIKE A POLAROID PHOTO DEVELOPING

THE V

STAY INSIDE THE V

When we're creating anew and our ideas are developing, we must be highly alert to suggestions that can take us off track.

Early on in my process of crafting a new keynote, I told a close colleague about my vision. He brightened and encouraged me to include a few references that he was convinced would help make my material stronger. His was a smart suggestion. And yet, I was back and forth on it.

I mentioned this in a conversation with the performer and director Frank Oz.

"Be careful of good ideas," Frank said.

Holding his hands together with the base of his palms touching and his fingers reaching forward like a snowplow forming a "V" shape, he explained . . .

"Here is your vision."
He indicated the space inside the V.

"If someone
suggests an
idea that's
really bad,
it's way
out here.
You know this
suggestion
is not an
option.
The idea
is too
far away from
your vision."

"But the
dangerous
ideas are the
good ones—
those that are
just outside."

TOO FAR OUT . . .
NOWHERE NEAR THE V

HMMMM. THAT'S A
GOOD IDEA

"What happens then is we say, 'Yehhh—that's pretty good.' And we adjust our vision a bit."

He pivoted his hands ever so slightly, redirecting the V.

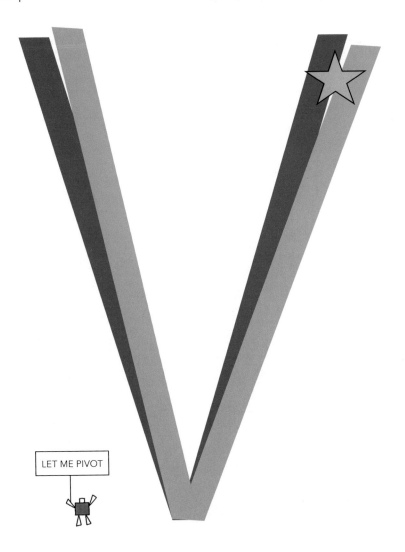

LET ME PIVOT

"Then another idea comes that's also a *good* idea, just barely outside the V. You adjust some more. Bit by bit, you get off course. And pretty soon it's not your vision anymore."

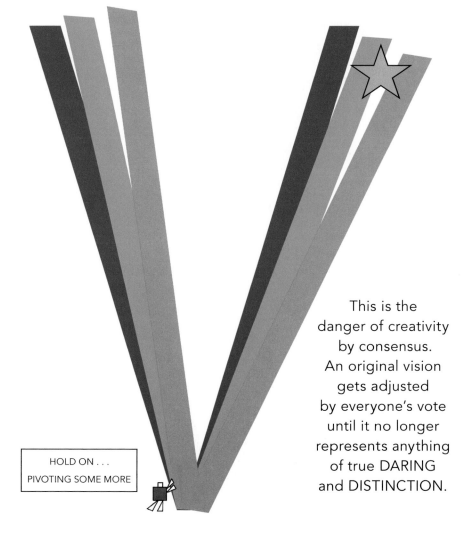

This is the danger of creativity by consensus. An original vision gets adjusted by everyone's vote until it no longer represents anything of true DARING and DISTINCTION.

HOLD ON . . .
PIVOTING SOME MORE

So now it's gone from this . . .

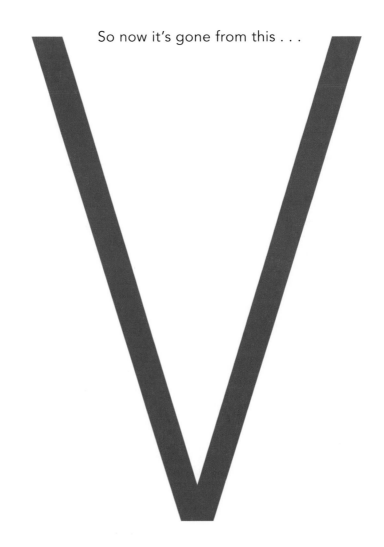

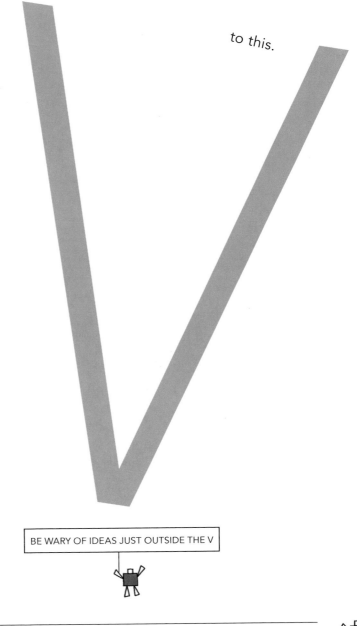

to this.

BE WARY OF IDEAS JUST OUTSIDE THE V

MAKE YOUR OWN MISTAKES

"I would rather follow my instincts and make a mistake than follow someone else's instincts and make a mistake. If you follow someone else's instincts and fail, you've failed and it's not even your own. At the end of the day, you want ownership even over your mistakes. And for that matter, I'll go even further. I'd rather follow my own instincts and fail than follow someone else's instincts and succeed." — Frank Oz

Risking forward requires being willing to make mistakes.

ADVICE

EVALUATE INPUT

"Re-examine all you have been told . . .
dismiss whatever insults your own soul."

— Walt Whitman

It's extraordinary how frequently people will offer an opinion, even when you haven't asked for one.

Whenever advice arrives in your orbit—solicited or not—you must filter it carefully.

Here are three variables to consider:

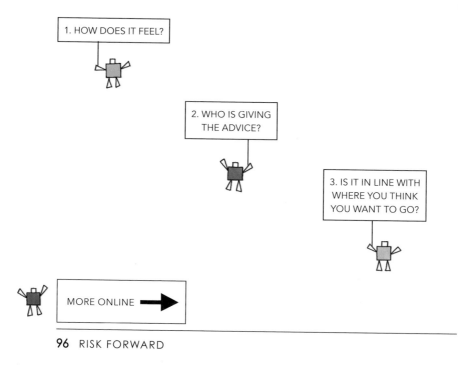

1. HOW DOES IT FEEL?

2. WHO IS GIVING THE ADVICE?

3. IS IT IN LINE WITH WHERE YOU THINK YOU WANT TO GO?

MORE ONLINE ➡

INSTINCTS

BE MORE YOU

During my years as an actor, I auditioned for a small part on the TV show *Sex and the City.*

I'd been called in for the role of a clinician—and I was jazzed.

In prep I asked a friend of mine who had been on the show for any insights she could offer. She asked what I planned to wear. My answer: a practical outfit—maybe a button-down collared shirt and slacks.

My friend's reply: "Look as hot as you can."

"Really? But I'm supposed to be a clinician."

"Victoria—it's called **Sex** *and the City.*"

Okayyyy, I thought.

A few days later, I showed up at the audition wearing a tight, royal blue, deep cut V-neck shirt. I read the lines for the clinician's role, and when I was done, the producer looked to the rest of the team.

"Let's have her read for Denise instead."

Whatttt? I thought to myself. Having gotten an advance peek at the script, I knew the Denise character was described as "the sexy restaurant hostess whose breasts pour out of her skimpy outfit."

Me? Not really. But I had no time to prepare. I had to Risk Forward.

YIKES . . .

I was nervous, and so as I delivered the lines, I covered my discomfort with sarcasm and a bit of sass. To my surprise, my delivery cracked up the team.

Even more to my surprise, a few days later, the casting director called to say I'd landed the part.

Because I hadn't had time to think about what a "sexy restaurant hostess" would sound like, I'd acted from the inside out, from a pure impulse within. I played the part in an original way—mostly as me, just with more attitude. The delivery had been unpredictable, against type, and funny. It surprised them. And it worked.

Film shooting was meant to take place a few weeks later, but for a number of reasons it was delayed. I used this window to prepare further, going over my meager five lines again and again, imagining what a sexy hostess might look like from the outside in. I developed a swinging walk and a sultry voice.

When production finally started again, I was driven down to Atlantic City to the Taj Mahal casino where we were to film. And when late at night it finally came time to shoot my scene, with my hair piled on my head and my makeup done, I was primed.

The lighting was set. The four lead women were seated. The camera was placed, lens focused, film rolling. The director called out, "Annnddd . . . action!"

I sauntered into frame, my arm looped around the male character Richard, and with all the sexiness I could muster, I delivered my lines.

The scene played out, and when it was complete, John, the director, called out, "Cut!" He walked to where we were all situated.

"Great. Good take." He nodded to everyone. "Let's do it again." Then he turned to me and said quietly, "Victoria—just be more you." He walked back to his place.

Camera rolling again, John called out: "Annnnd . . . action!" I sauntered in, trying out a slightly more Victoria-style voice, but I could feel myself being halfway between my sexy pre-planned character (outside in) and my original audition version (inside out).

"Cut!" Once again, John made his way over. "Victoria—let's try it again. Just be more you."

I cringed. Months of rehearsing on my own had solidified my behavior in a way that was hard to change.

We did the scene a few more times, and with each take, I felt like I fell short.

The creative team had cast me originally because I didn't re-enact the stereotypical syrupy sexy waitress. Instead, I was wry and smart and sassy—honest impulses that came from within.

But during all the months when production was on hold, I hadn't trusted that my original approach had been enough. I had tried to become what I thought they wanted me to be.

Risking forward comes from within.

HONOR YOUR INSTINCTS

ACTION

DON'T JUST DO SOMETHING

When I first started learning about improvisational theater, I thought the best way to participate and contribute was to remain highly active, speaking and being physically expressive in every scene. I was zealous and energetic. I thought I was playing full out.

Patricia Ryan Madson, an absolutely superb teacher, offered me this guidance.

"Don't just do something, stand there."

As she explained, new improvisers make the mistake of jumping into the scene without first recognizing the dynamics at play. They think they must "do" something, assuming any action is better than none. This happens in the improvisational realms of business and life as well.

People . . .

- speak up in meetings just to talk.
- start certain projects because everyone else in their field is doing them.
- react too quickly to an issue without first taking the time to find out more about what actually happened
  . . . and why.

As my friend Joe Calloway says, "Just 'doing something' is not a good strategy."

SOMETIMES RISKING FORWARD
LOOKS LIKE STANDING STILL

INDECISION

DECISIVENESS IS OVERRATED

There's a pervasive belief that decisiveness is inherently good and that indecisiveness is a negative trait—a character flaw.

For anyone who may be finding themselves in the throes of indecision, the inclination is to mask it, fearing you will reveal a weakness.

But how valuable is decisiveness if the result is a poor decision?

When we're put under pressure, we tend to bypass doing our due diligence—whether we're hiring someone, purchasing a product, planning a trip, or making a choice on where to invest our time, talents, or dollars.

I made this mistake a number of times in my business when a partner on a potential venture was pressuring me. To appear clearheaded and decisive, I said, "Okay. Yes, let's do it." That one "yes" led to months of a misguided use of my time, stress, lost money, and significant opportunity costs.

I could have simply said, "I need another few days. It's too important a decision to rush."

My client Kate Hutchison calls this "Strategic Procrastination."

THE ICEBERG OF INDECISION

When people are pressuring you to "just make a decision," they're often focused on one piece only.

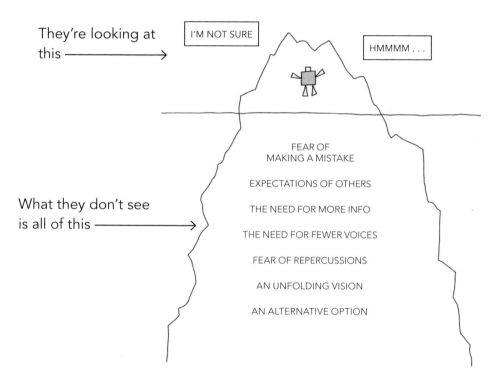

They're looking at this ⟶

I'M NOT SURE

HMMMM . . .

What they don't see is all of this ⟶

FEAR OF
MAKING A MISTAKE

EXPECTATIONS OF OTHERS

THE NEED FOR MORE INFO

THE NEED FOR FEWER VOICES

FEAR OF REPERCUSSIONS

AN UNFOLDING VISION

AN ALTERNATIVE OPTION

These are the buried reasons, the deeper issues and underwater currents that live far below.

MORE ONLINE ➡

RESPECT YOUR INDECISION

Indecision often carries wisdom.

One of the greatest gifts we can give people when they're struggling with a decision is our patience and compassion . . . and if they reach out for help, to ask questions that will help them discover their *own* answers and recognize the value of their *own* ideas.

This is also one of the greatest gifts we can give to ourselves.

Examine why you might be hesitant.

Ask yourself . . .

- Why might this *not* be right?
- What could be a better alternative?
- What am I not admitting?
- What are the implications of this decision?
- What does this represent?
- Who can help?

Search for clues to your own Inner Current and pay attention when you find them.

We sometimes think that when we make the right decision there will be clangs of affirmation ringing in our head, but it's actually the opposite: there's silence. The noise subsides.

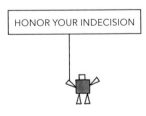

HONOR YOUR INDECISION

JUST
BECAUSE

JUST BECAUSE
YOU'RE GOOD
AT SOMETHING
DOESN'T MEAN
YOU HAVE TO DO IT

JUST BECAUSE
YOU HAVE AN OFFER
DOESN'T MEAN
YOU HAVE TO TAKE IT

JUST BECAUSE
YOU'RE NOT GOOD
AT SOMETHING AT THE START
DOESN'T MEAN YOU'RE
NOT MEANT TO DO IT

JUST BECAUSE
EVERYONE ELSE
THINKS IT'S A GOOD IDEA
DOESN'T MEAN
IT'S RIGHT FOR YOU

JUST BECAUSE
NO ONE ELSE
IS DOING IT
DOESN'T MEAN
IT'S A BAD IDEA

JUST BECAUSE
YOU HAVEN'T
WORKED ON IT
IN A WHILE
DOESN'T MEAN
YOU'RE NOT MEANT
TO DO IT

MORE ONLINE ➡

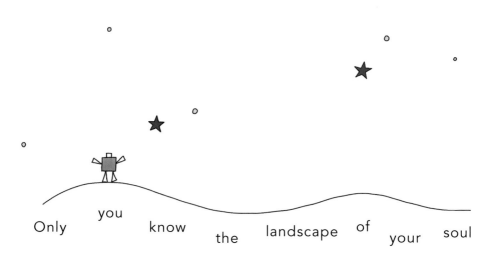

Only you know the landscape of your soul

5 MYTHS

MISCONCEPTIONS

As you Risk Forward, it's essential to remain alert to long-standing conventional myths.

These myths are sometimes touted as truths, requirements that you must master in order to be successful.

While they can propel you forward, they can also become the very barriers that hold you back and block your Inner Current.

THE MYTH OF PURPOSE

There's a lot of talk about "finding your purpose."

But you don't need to find your purpose.

Your "purpose" is already in you.

Finding the words to describe it may take some time, but if you keep following what pulls you forward and lights you up, you'll be on the right track.

**YOU DON'T HAVE TO NAME YOUR PURPOSE
TO BE LIVING YOUR PURPOSE.**

THE MYTH OF GOALS

For many people, goal setting is taken as an unquestionably positive activity and a requirement for success.

But if you think back on your life, it's likely many of your top experiences arrived without you ever having set a goal for them.

While goal setting certainly has its place, it can also lead you astray. Unless your goals are aligned with your Inner Current, they will take you

WAY

OFF

COURSE.

Sometimes goals are born out of "goal contagion," where we unconsciously adopt other people's definition of success as our own. Look closely at your goals. Are they really yours? What is success . . . for you?

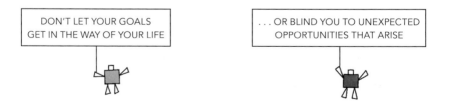

| DON'T LET YOUR GOALS GET IN THE WAY OF YOUR LIFE | . . . OR BLIND YOU TO UNEXPECTED OPPORTUNITIES THAT ARISE |

GOAL SETTING CAN LEAD YOU ASTRAY.

THE MYTH OF FOCUS

There's a commonly held belief that in order to achieve anything of meaning or merit, you must have focus.

But "focus" is frequently misinterpreted to mean you must express yourself through one core activity and aim your efforts at one main outcome only.

For those who have a range of disparate talents and interests, making a choice like this is a painful and counterproductive proposition.

Some people express themselves in one main direction. Others express themselves in a variety of ways.

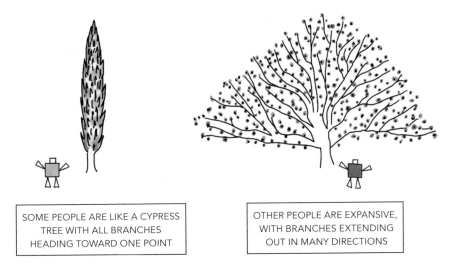

SOME PEOPLE ARE LIKE A CYPRESS
TREE WITH ALL BRANCHES
HEADING TOWARD ONE POINT

OTHER PEOPLE ARE EXPANSIVE,
WITH BRANCHES EXTENDING
OUT IN MANY DIRECTIONS

FOCUS COMES IN MANY FORMS.

THE MYTH OF FOLLOWERS

There's a misconception that the more followers you have, the greater your value.

NUMBERS DO NOT EQUATE WITH VALUE.

THE MYTH OF SPEED

There's a general philosophy that faster is always better. And while we know it's not, many of us live with a constant sense of urgency. It can wreak havoc on our inner lives.

I often think back to a moment with Marcel Marceau when he was teaching us about movement and rhythm.

I was standing onstage in the empty rehearsal theater, having just presented a short five-minute performance piece. Marceau arrived at my side to offer his critique.

I braced myself, sucking in air to bolster my spirit. Had I been too slow? Did I take too much time? I had tried to be quick.

Marceau squinted at me, leaning in and placing his face close to mine. He whispered, "Donnn't rush. Trust yourself, your own rhythm, your own internal timing."

It was a lesson he taught me again and again. "Breeeathe, Victoria. Breeeeathe."

Risking forward is not about speed. It's about having the courage to respect your own rhythm, even when the whole cry of voices is telling you something else.

We must honor our own internal clocks . . .

EVERYONE DEVELOPS IN THEIR OWN WAY

. . . AND ON THEIR OWN SCHEDULE

FASTER IS NOT NECESSARILY BETTER.

MINDSET

In the course of any given day, no matter what hour it is, you may think you are screwing up in some way.

YOU WON'T
MAKE IT

OTHERS ARE
AHEAD

YOU DON'T
HAVE WHAT
IT TAKES

WHAT WERE
YOU
THINKING?

YOU'LL NEVER
GET IT RIGHT

THE CLOCK
OF ANGST

WHAT'S THE
POINT?

YOU
MESSED
UP

GET IT
TOGETHER

IT'S NOT GOING
TO WORK

IT'S NOT
WORTH IT

YOU SHOULD
HAVE STARTED
SOONER

HOW WILL
YOU
CATCH UP?

There is an alternative.

BREEEATHE

TRUST
YOURSELF

STAY
PRESENT

YOU HAVE
WHAT IT
TAKES

BE GENTLE
WITH
YOURSELF

THE CLOCK
OF CALM

YOU'VE
GOT THIS

TRUST YOUR
PACE

IT'S OK
TO PAUSE

EVERYONE'S
ON THEIR OWN
CLOCK

YOU'LL
FIGURE IT OUT

YOU'RE
DOING GREAT

HONOR
YOUR
INSTINCTS

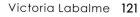

QUITTING

YOU CAN TAKE A BREAK

At one point in my career when I'd had a particularly tough stretch, I reached a phase where I figured maybe I should quit performing. I loved it, it lit me up, but it was such a challenging road at times.

During that period, I was fortunate enough to have a desk in an office on Broadway. Jim Freydberg, a Broadway producer, supported about five artists each year by giving them a work space at his headquarters in Times Square.

Exasperated, I slumped in a leather chair in Jim's office and told him I was done.

I looked out the window down at the blinking lights of Broadway. This life of writing and creating my own work wasn't for me.

With a mass of papers on his desk and framed show posters behind him, Jim looked up at me through his blue-tinted glasses.

"You can take a break, but you can't quit."

This option had never occurred to me.

In our "all or nothing" world, the combination of the two together offered a whole new approach to risking forward.

We don't have to be pushing all. the. time.

MORE ONLINE

DETOURS

THE DETOUR AND THE PATH

There are times in your life when you may take a turn that can appear to be a total detour.

Situations arise that you couldn't have anticipated.

Occasionally, too, you agree to do something that takes you off the path you thought you were on.

You might be disappointed in yourself because you didn't stay on course; you might think you didn't have what it took to Risk Forward.

Or . . . you can see that the detour could be your true path.

The story line of your life may not always be what you expected.

In *Muppet Guys Talking*, a documentary I co-produced, Jerry Nelson—creator of iconic characters such as Count von Count and Mr. Snuffleupagus—recalls his life's journey. He shares how he had planned to be an actor and had instead ended up as a puppeteer. As he talks about the incredible unexpected opportunities this path brought him, he reflects back to his very early days as an actor and acknowledges, "I'm not who I thought I was back then."

Sometimes in risking forward we find out who we really are.

A DETOUR
IS ONLY A DETOUR
IF YOU SEE IT
AS A DETOUR

SURRENDERING

RISKING FORWARD
IS NOT A STRAIGHT LINE

It has its own course, its own design.

At times the path may look daunting,

twisting in unexpected ways and doubling back.

Have patience.

Have courage.

Keep going.

RISKING FORWARD CAN
BE A WILD RIDE

Like Space Mountain, Disney World's iconic roller-coaster that travels through the dark, when you're risking forward, there are 20-foot drops and hairpin turns.

And you don't see them coming.

It's amazing how we cackle with glee when it's an amusement park ride. We love the surprise and the unexpected turns; we even pay money for the experience.

This is good to remember.

Risking forward is an adventure.

COURAGE

THE POET'S WISDOM

Early in my career, I had a chance to meet W. S. Merwin, one of my favorite poets.

I had been working as an intern at a literary magazine called *The Paris Review*, and because the current edition featured one of Merwin's poems, the editor wanted to send him a copy as soon as the batch came in from the printer.

Merwin's apartment was not far from our headquarters, and so, on the off chance that I'd get to meet the legendary poet, I volunteered to make the delivery myself.

When I rang the bell at his home, the door swung open and there Merwin stood: white hair, gentle smile, soft blue eyes.

With a bow of his head, he thanked me and invited me in.

I was beside myself. Here I was in Merwin's home.

The visit is dreamlike now, a collection of blurred images

   . . . me sitting perched on his living room couch

   . . . the room feeling blue—was it the rug, or possibly the drapes?

   . . . his asking about my life and my work.

And as I spilled my struggles over not knowing what was next, his eyes seemed illuminated from behind, almost phosphorescent, as if he could see through me.

And when I left, halfway down the darkened hall, I turned back to see him standing at his door.

He smiled, clutched a hand to his heart, then thrust his fist skyward, and with the touch of a French accent—as if to send a soldier off—he declared,

"Couuurahhhhge! Couuurahhhhge!"

FEAR

EVERYONE IS SCARED
AT SOME POINT

. . . even the people who say they're not, actually occasionally are.

Everyone is dealing with their own pressures, conflicts, and concerns.

So be kind

—to them, to yourself—because no one has it all together all the time.

No one.

YOUR NOBLE INTENT

NOBILITY

There's a question I have asked thousands of people around the world to offer perspective and help them reconnect with the meaning in what they do.

I call it my Noble Intent question.

And it is this:

"What is the nobility behind your work?"

When I asked this question of Dave Goelz, one of the original Muppet performers, he responded with an answer I never saw coming.

"The nobility behind the work?" Dave repeated back.

He chuckled, and then without hesitation he replied, "Folly. It's human folly. And the degree to which we're all lost."

There is nobility in not always knowing the way and yet having the courage to Risk Forward.

YOUR
HIDDEN
LEGACY

EVERYONE LEAVES A LEGACY

There might be times when you wonder if what you're doing even matters.

You might look around to see others who have done more, made more, built more, or become more recognized.

But you can't measure legacy.

In every area of this earth, people are setting legacies in motion without even realizing it.

They are inspiring a student, leading a group, raising a child, designing a campaign, supporting a friend, teaching a course, running an experiment, helping their team, coaching a client, or creating new work . . .

Their names may not be widely recognized, but their contributions are significant.

We may never know the full effects of their actions or our own . . . but we can do this: we can follow what lights us up; express our insights; speak our truth; and stand for what is right.

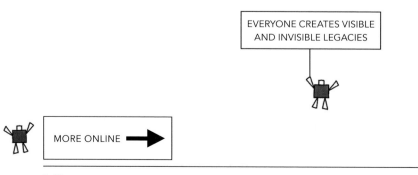

EVERYONE CREATES VISIBLE
AND INVISIBLE LEGACIES

MORE ONLINE

Imagine one person you influence . . .

goes on to influence others . . .

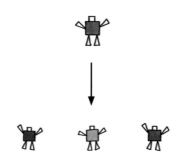

and they in turn influence still more . . .

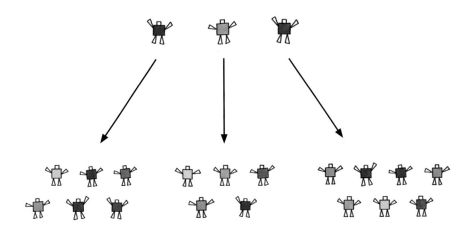

creating an impact beyond comprehension.

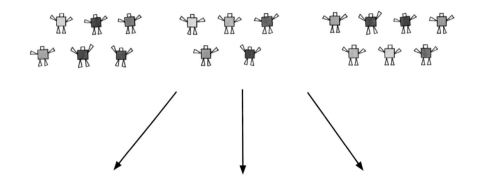

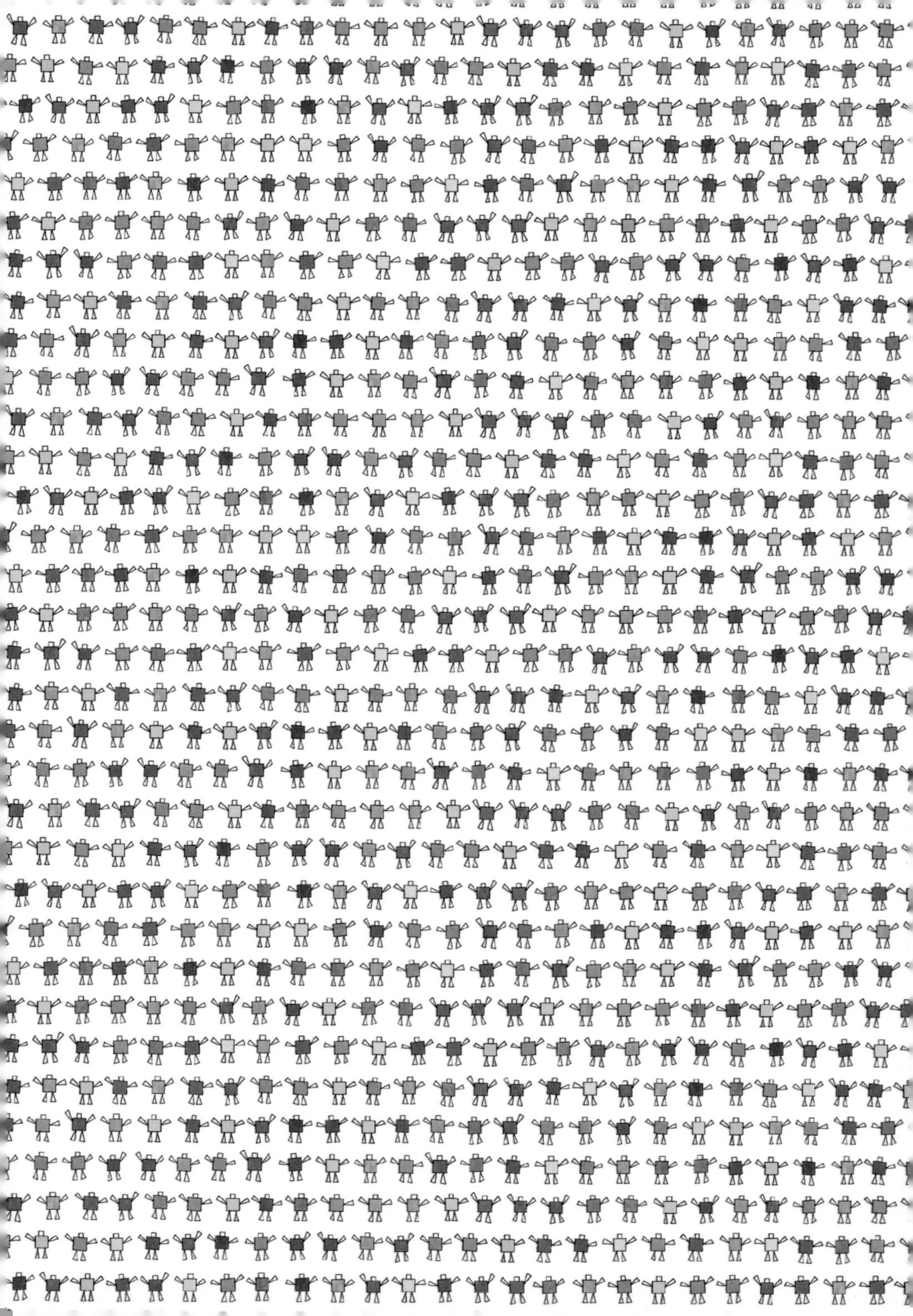

Your legacy is infinite and immeasurable.

Long after you're gone,

like the light from a star that has since left the sky,

your legacy will continue to travel

through time and space for centuries—

influencing people

in ways you can't imagine now,

reaching souls

you may never know.

OH! I JUST HAD A WISP
OF A THOUGHT,
A GLIMMER
OF AN IDEA

YOUR
LIFE'S
WORK

The day after my mother was diagnosed with pancreatic cancer, we gathered at our family's home in Connecticut.

As the evening arrived and the light began to dim, my mother went outside and walked to the edge of our property, gathering evergreen branches, twigs, and flowers from her garden.

Back in the house, she laid everything out on the hearth and stood before an open vase up on the mantel. Piece by piece, she began to create a bouquet.

She did this every Friday evening and always referred to it as her "Life's Work."

I flopped down on the oversized living room chair, my legs dangling over the edge, and I watched her moving as if she were conducting a silent orchestra, sliding stems into the vase, then gently lifting them back up into position.

Recognizing that she would be gone in a matter of months, I realized I never quite understood why she called this her "Life's Work." And so I asked.

Branch in one hand, cutters in the other, she turned toward me . . .

"When I was appointed to be on the board of a corporation, I was the only woman who held a seat. The men on the board asked me to give a speech to the company—how did I get to where I am in my life: a Ph.D., a published author, associate director of an institute, four children . . . because I never had a Five-Year Plan. I always just did what was next as best I could. And then the metaphor I came up with was this, and this is the story I told:

'Every Friday, as my family gathers in the evening at our home, in the dying light of the day, I go around the house and find what I can—a pine bough, a twig, some flowers. And with that, I make a bouquet.

I do my best with what I've got. This is my Life's Work.'"

She pivoted back and continued conducting.

A branch arched off to the left; a stalk with purple flowers jutted to the right.

"I like how it's not symmetrical," I murmured.

"Yes," she nodded. "Things should be *not perfect.*"

DO THE BEST WITH WHAT YOU'VE GOT

So trust your Inner Current,

your insights and ideas,

and the Crimson Star . . .

even if you're not sure where it all will lead.

The courage to head into the unknown

is the starting point

of all great art and science,

great entrepreneurship and enterprise

. . . and great lives.

Risk Forward.

Why?

Because you . . .

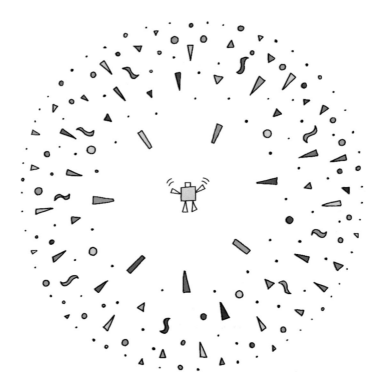

. . . are a wonder.

AFTERWORD

The process of writing this book was itself a Risk Forward.

Many people questioned me. Why this book and not that one? What's your goal?

I started to question myself.

Sometimes the path went sideways or seemingly backwards.

There were moments of confusion, so I followed my curiosity.

There were moments when I wanted to quit, and I took a break.

There were moments when I almost outsourced my vision, and I returned to my own.

Moments when I wondered about my reach, and I remembered one soul.

Along the way, I came face-to-face with every challenge this book addresses.

I lived through the Fog of Not Knowing again and again.

There's a misconception floating around that a "guide" only makes the journey once and then never faces the challenges again.

The truth is, we walk the path many times . . . just in a new form and in a new way.

Each time through, we trust the Inner Current a little more.

And each time through, the light of the Crimson Star becomes a bit more familiar.

RESOURCES AND NEXT STEPS

I'm so glad this book found its way to you.

Risk Forward is an experience that continues.

For additional stories, videos, journal pages, and "how to" steps . . . and to learn about our Risk Forward community, go to www.RiskForward.com/Resources

I'll see you there.

—V

ACKNOWLEDGMENTS

First and foremost, a profound thanks to Reid Tracy and Patty Gift for saying YES to this project . . . and to the entire Hay House family for supporting this vision. To my editor extraordinaire, Anne Barthel, for your ever-gracious, open-minded, and skilled, steady guidance. I couldn't have done this without you. To the core book support team: Hillary Bradley, Blake Fly, Micheline Auger, Annie Hyman Pratt, and Lisa Labalme Osterland. Your unfailing encouragement, texts, calls, and emails from Day 1 along with your insights and perspective on various drafts buoyed me throughout. This book would not exist without your belief in it. To Michelle Falzon for giving your time so generously and offering masterful support at every key step along the way. To Seth Barrish for your invaluable input helping me refine the manuscript in the final weeks. To Ashley Zink for your outstanding and wide-ranging talents, including helping design the cover. To the Eagle Nest Creative group for literally walking through the manuscript with me and providing feedback as I laid the pages out across my grandmother's art studio floor. To Kate Medina for your no-BS advice and savvy guidance. To Bill O'Hanlon for our many calls and your wise counsel on the book-writing experience. To Steven Pressfield for your world-class friendship and our conversations over these many years about the creative process. To the Risk Forward® Special Experience group and Rock The Room® group: thank you for embracing these concepts early on, for your delight in the material, and for sharing your incredible results in our sessions and online communities. To the PAC/Performing Arts Collective for your shrewd insights and kindness as I presented my new work: Mike Birbiglia, Lewis Black, Derek DelGaudio, Mary Karr, Jen Stein, Chris Wink, and Alan Zweibel. To my readers who combed through my early "seedling" manuscripts and sent back detailed, perceptive notes: Ted Schillinger, Joe Calloway, Madeleine Homan Blanchard, Nancy Duarte, Nina Houghton, Kate Hutchison, Eve Labalme, Sarah Mack, Tracy Burke, Lee Brock, Oliver Curtis, Mary Jane Dykeman, Jonathan R. Stein, Albert Torres, Pete Docter, Andy Nyman, Stan Slap, Raakhee Mirchandani, and Patricia Ryan Madson. Your suggestions made a difference. Thanks to those who provided specific, unexpected support along the way: Clint Greenleaf, Marc Baird, Sally Hogshead, Gregg Goldston, Peter Wisch, Mastin Kipp, Will Hamilton, John Gallagher, Stu McLaren, Jill Angelo, Sonia Simone, Jason Friedman, Lynne Hale, Henry Labalme, Jenny Labalme, Edith Pepper, Dan Truman, Taylor McFerran, Matt Robinson, Elie Docter, Melinda Cohan, Shannon Forman, Brian McDonald, Charlie Melcher, Rich McFarland, Ann Wilson, Julie Ann Cairns, and my friends in the JW Plat Plus Group who showed up in numerous ways. A special thanks to Tricia Breidenthal and Bryn Starr Best for your professionalism and care in all aspects of the design and in recreating my original layout; and Ruby Falzon, for your adept and attentive help with the Little Works® characters and colors. To my father, George Labalme, for your unflagging belief in and love of these ideas; and my mother, Patricia Labalme, for your elegance and your graceful life philosophy of letting things unfold. To my stepchildren—Cody, Hudson, Cooper, and Hadley—you inspire me in ways you don't even know. Last and most importantly of all, immeasurable thanks to my best friend, highest creative bar, and inimitable husband, Frank Oz. You studied every draft and offered stunning feedback. As I said when we wed, "With you I risk my heart forward . . . and it is safe."

THANK YOU ALL...SO VERY MUCH

ABOUT VICTORIA

Victoria Labalme helps people perform at their highest levels in work, onstage, on camera, and in life. Her unconventional approach offers a surprising blend of art and business.

As a member of the Speaker Hall of Fame, Victoria is known for her keynotes and workshops around the world. Her proprietary systems and strategies have been embraced by more than 700 organizations and top teams at Starbucks, Microsoft, Intel, Verizon, Coca-Cola, Cisco, Oracle, Chase, Lowe's, L'Oreal, Omnicom, PayPal, American Heart Association, MetLife, Canada Life, Workday, Optum, Blue Cross Blue Shield, the World Bank, universities, cultural institutions, and not-for-profits.

Victoria has been the trusted consultant to C-suite executives, leading entrepreneurs, and *New York Times* best-selling authors. She has coached hundreds of elite individuals for high-stakes presentations including keynotes, live streams, PBS Specials, Oprah's SuperSoul Session, and arena events.

Her projects have received critical acclaim from *The Hollywood Reporter, Variety*, BBC, CBS, *Los Angeles Times*, and *Good Morning America.*

Victoria is the founder of Risk Forward® and Rock The Room®—a full suite of products designed to help individuals and organizations uncover their original ideas and express them with the unexpected twist that distinguishes their work.

To learn more about her keynotes, events, virtual experiences, and private consulting, please visit:

www.VictoriaLabalme.com
www.RiskForward.com
www.RockTheRoom.com

We hope you enjoyed this Hay House book. If you'd like to receive our online catalog featuring additional information on Hay House books and products, or if you'd like to find out more about the Hay Foundation, please contact:

Hay House, Inc., P.O. Box 5100, Carlsbad, CA 92018-5100
(760) 431-7695 or (800) 654-5126
(760) 431-6948 (fax) or (800) 650-5115 (fax)
www.hayhouse.com® • www.hayfoundation.org

———

Published in Australia by: Hay House Australia Pty. Ltd.,
18/36 Ralph St., Alexandria NSW 2015
Phone: 612-9669-4299 • *Fax:* 612-9669-4144
www.hayhouse.com.au

Published in the United Kingdom by: Hay House UK, Ltd.,
The Sixth Floor, Watson House, 54 Baker Street, London W1U 7BU
Phone: +44 (0)20 3927 7290 • *Fax:* +44 (0)20 3927 7291
www.hayhouse.co.uk

Published in India by: Hay House Publishers India,
Muskaan Complex, Plot No. 3, B-2, Vasant Kunj, New Delhi 110 070
Phone: 91-11-4176-1620 • *Fax:* 91-11-4176-1630
www.hayhouse.co.in

———

Access New Knowledge.
Anytime. Anywhere.

Learn and evolve at your own pace
with the world's leading experts.

www.hayhouseU.com